ISBN-13: 978-1545599020
ISBN-10: 1545599025

The Essence of Nature

By: Latosha Pahn-Lee

Nature is an adventure!

Love

Live

Explore

Adventures

Outdoors

With

Nature

At

No

Cost.

Hello! If you are reading this, you have either purchased or rented my book. I would like to personally thank each of you. You have helped to make my book a success. God has blessed me so that I am able to present to you a book that will help you relax and become one with nature. Go ahead grab some tea and a big of chips. Whatever you prefer, get it, and find a nice place to read and enjoy!

Each and everyday we
experience life. It could be
your daily experience with
people, a pet, or some other
form of life, we encounter.
As you look around yourself,
you will see that life is
everywhere. The picture of
the moth was an act of good
timing, and having my
camera at the right place, at
the right time. There is so
much to explore outdoors.

Many people do not
enjoy the buzzing insects
while they are outdoors, but I
cherish each moment outside.
There is always something
exciting to see and explore.

"Wake up and see the world, Nature lives. "

Every day, we live and we also learn. Sometimes our brains get overworked, and we get frustrated. It is at that time that we should consider taking a break, or resting. Stress is a part of many of our daily lives. Many people may go on vacation, go to the park, exercise, read a book, among many other things, to release stress. Whatever your ideal stress reliever may be, consider doing it from time to time. It is essential to your health and your mind!

"Color soothes the soul!"
Keep quite so that you don't
scare this little guy away!
That is what I told myself as I
quietly snapped this photo.
The attractive color of this
lizard is stunning. It gives
you the feel of being
outdoors. There are so many
different colors, sizes, and
types of lizards'. If you love
lizards, the flower garden
setting, is perfect for you.

This adorable little pup is named Ruby! There is nothing like having a loyal pet. However, I do not take her along when I am doing photography, simply because she runs away all the amazing wildlife images that I can capture. She is a courageous little puppy.

I call this little guy Star! Each
morning he lands here,
singing his little heart out.
There is nothing like a free
performance!

Now Ruby has gotten older and she is very smart. I have spent as many hours needed, to get Ruby ready for programs and other activities. She is one of the smartest dogs I've seen yet. When she is outside, I will leave her a bottled water. She will then chew a small hole around the bottle top or the neck of the bottle, so that she can have a drink of water.

The color of the sunflower is

the color that I most admire.

The way in which the

sunflower grows is unique.

There is always plenty to see
when you are around water.
There are so many creatures
flying around and floating in
the water. It is a wonderful
place to relax. The sound of
water itself is relaxing to the
mind.

"When the seasons change,
the blooms of the flower
change."

I love seeing the kids at my
gatherings as they attack the
dessert tray. Today I have a
variety of all sorts of treats so
that the children can indulge
as they please! Children are
the future, so why not reward
them every now and then
with a little something. Their
smiling faces and little
conversations are priceless.

When you hear the word nature, you may begin to think of the trees and the flowers that surround us. There are so many more concepts to nature then you may believe. When you are outdoors, you can do just about anything. We all remember being outdoors as a child, playing and getting dirty. We had wild imaginations that were creative.

Wherever Red goes, the hens
are never far behind.

There are many paths that
you will have to take to
become successful. I know
that if you believe in God and
yourself, you can accomplish
anything. All it takes is
concentration and dedication.
"Each day that the sun shines,
thank God, fore he has given
us light."

"Life has many up's and down's. As we grow older and wiser, we will begin to understand life, and accept the true meaning. Love yourself, as well as your neighbor. Life is love, and love is life." Enjoy each of your days to the fullest!

Just imagine a nice walk
through the flower garden.
Do you hear the buzzing
sound from the nearby
insects? The wind is calmly
blowing through your hair.
Now inhale and exhale, and
allow your mind to be at
ease. How do you feel? Now
look at your surroundings.
Everything is so colorful and
captivating to the eye.

Buck-y, is a pleasure to be
around. He is older now, but
still adorable. There is
nothing like the sweet
country sound of a southern
farm.

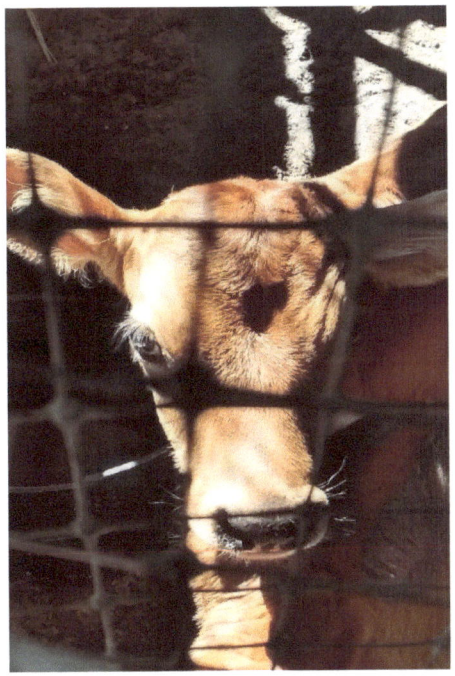

Did someone say dinner
time? Watch out, here they
come.

It looks like
someone got
caught taking
a bath!

This guy comes along with
nature. I am so glad that he
can't get inside.

Here piggy, piggy, come and get it!

Wildlife is one of the main resources of food. Eating is necessary, but what we eat varies, from person to person. It is relaxing to explore the many adventures that come along with being outdoors. Let's not forget some of these unpleasant smells.

The creative garden, collard
greens and tomatoes!

We have Popcorn on the farm
as our personal chicken
guard. He keeps away the
fox, and other unwelcomed
guests.

This is my very own southern
whipped banana pudding.

Be creative!

The shining Christmas lights
make it, "The most
wonderful time of the year!"

Roger the squirrel plays his
part on the fence. He now has
a family. I will continue to
monitor them as they grow
and expand their family. He
loves to play along the fence.
This is Roger's daily activity.

This is a very unique photo of
a mother hen and her new
born chicks.

It looks like rain is in the
forecast!

I finally caught the sun at
sunrise! This is surely not my
first time seeing it, but it is
my first time taking a picture
of it. Beautiful!

This is my very own onion patch. "With a little love and nourishment, you can get anything to grow."

English peas, so pretty and green! There are no pesticides added to this garden.

The roller pigeon is a bird that I admire. You will never know which way this fellow will fly. As he flies off high up in the sky, he does tricks. Now that's something to see.

These are the sweetest
strawberries that I have ever
tasted! Locally grown by me!

Do you see the pigeon in the tree?

Diamond is all set. She loves her treats and she's not sharing!

It looks like a storm is
approaching.

Whenever I am outdoors,
there goes Roger. He is not
frightened of me. I have been
coming out each day to greet
him, and to leave him some
food. Sometimes he allows
me to take a picture or two.

Small, but captivating!

My little southern peach tree!

Lovely green
tomatoes dripping wet during
a light rain.

These are some more of my fine grown mouthwatering strawberries, yummy!

The squash this year is
growing like wildflowers.

Creativity!

This is Sugarfoot. She was my very first pet. Although she is no longer with us, her spirit lives on.

There is nothing like summer time BBQ's. The aroma from the food cooking on the grill, reminds me of summer cookouts and gatherings!

Red blooms set the

atmosphere for a lovely day!

Ferns are always lovely to look at.

Spring colors, oh
what a wonderful site to see!

I love nature. Pets are also
apart of nature. I strive to
help save animals. They are
an important part of nature's
life cycle.

Ruby is ready for her fun filled day at the park. There you may find us walking or running along, side by side. When Ruby and I, are having our fun at the park, we are also bonding. Along with bonding we are keeping ourselves motivated and in shape. She also serves as my first line of defense just in case trouble comes. "Be dedicated to your pet, and your pet will be dedicated to you."

I hope that you enjoyed this picture filled book. This book was designed to relax your mind, and to show you a portion of what nature has to offer. I hope that I have achieved that goal. Thank you for reading!

Visit me at
authorlatoshapahn@
instagram.com